THE BIBLE COLORING BOOK

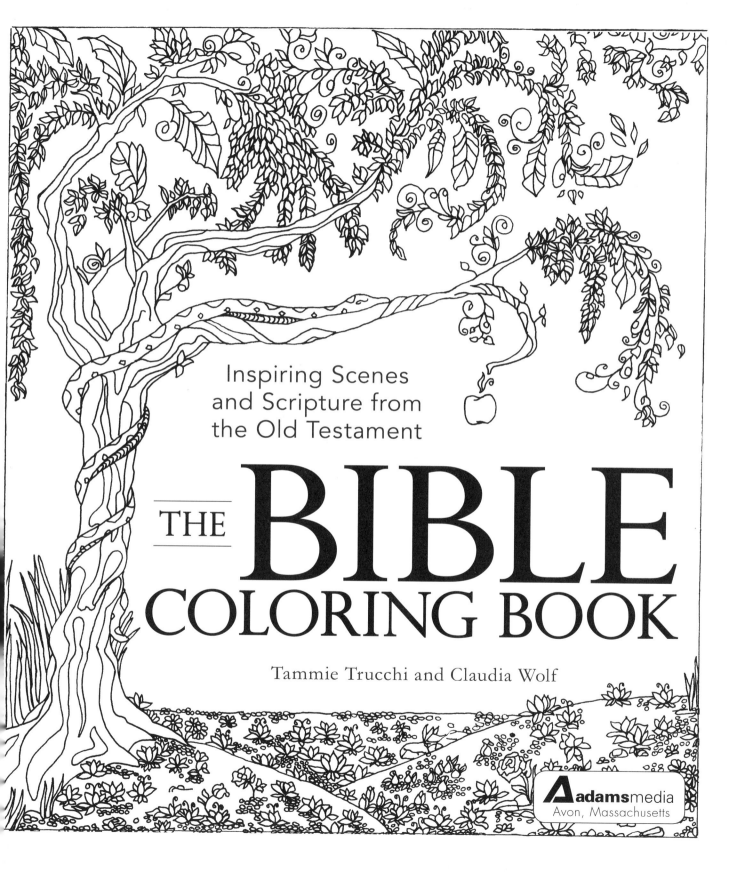

Inspiring Scenes
and Scripture from
the Old Testament

THE BIBLE
COLORING BOOK

Tammie Trucchi and Claudia Wolf

adamsmedia
Avon, Massachusetts

Published by
Adams Media, a division of F+W Media, Inc.
57 Littlefield Street, Avon, MA 02322. U.S.A.
www.adamsmedia.com

ISBN 10: 1-4405-9522-4
ISBN 13: 978-1-4405-9522-6
Printed in the United States of America.

10   9   8   7   6   5   4   3   2

Scripture quotations are from the Holy Bible, King James Version.

Cover design by Erin Alexander.
Cover and interior illustrations by Tammie Trucchi and Claudia Wolf.

This book is available at quantity discounts for bulk purchases.
For information, please call 1-800-289-0963.

INTRODUCTION

The stories of the Bible have inspired people for ages. Now they can be your source of creative inspiration as you color in scenes and scripture from the Old Testament. Whether featuring a verse from Proverbs or a picture of Moses parting the Red Sea, each coloring page lets you reflect on a Bible passage and enjoy the calming practice of coloring.

Colors are important symbols in the Bible and you can incorporate those symbols into your coloring. Bring life to the Garden of Eden by selecting lush greens; the color green was meant to represent life and growth in those descriptions. Royalty was often described as wearing purple, or having things in their courts made of fine materials dyed purple. That color therefore came to symbolize royalty and riches, and can be used when coloring in the scenes with King Solomon and the Queen of Sheba. Blue is often used to represent the heavenly realm and can be used to color the skies over many of these scenes, or the patterns in the stylized scripture. By combining these Biblical symbols with your own color choices, you'll be able to create beautiful, personalized depictions of your favorite Bible moments.

The Bible Coloring Book gives you the opportunity to reflect on your own life and blessings while enriching your knowledge and love of the Bible. It's a welcome celebration of your faith—and creativity!

The Garden of Eden · Illustration by Tammie Trucchi

Noah's Ark · Illustration by Tammie Trucchi

The Tower of Babel · Illustration by Tammie Trucchi

Lot's Wife · Illustration by Tammie Trucchi

Rebekah at the Well · Illustration by Tammie Trucchi

And, behold, I am with thee, AND will keep thee in all places whither thou goest. —GENESIS 28:15

Jacob, Leah, and Rachel · Illustration by Tammie Trucchi

Joseph's Coat of Many Colors · Illustration by Tammie Trucchi

Baby Moses · Illustration by Tammie Trucchi

Moses and the Burning Bush · Illustration by Tammie Trucchi

The Passover · Illustration by Tammie Trucchi

The Parting of the Red Sea · Illustration by Tammie Trucchi

I AM THE
Lord
THAT HEALETH
thee.
—EXODUS 15:26

Water from the Rock · Illustration by Tammie Trucchi

The Golden Calf · Illustration by Tammie Trucchi

My presence shall go with thee, and I will give thee rest. —EXODUS 33:14

Illustration by Claudia Wolf

Ye shall be holy; for I The Lord your God am holy.

—LEVITICUS 19:2

I WILL WALK AMONG YOU,
AND WILL BE YOUR
GOD,
AND YE SHALL BE MY PEOPLE.

—LEVITICUS 26:12

The Bronze Snake · Illustration by Tammie Trucchi

THOU SHALT

Love

THE LORD THY GOD
WITH ALL THINE

Heart,

AND WITH
ALL THY

Soul,

AND WITH
ALL THY

Might.

—DEUTERONOMY 6:5

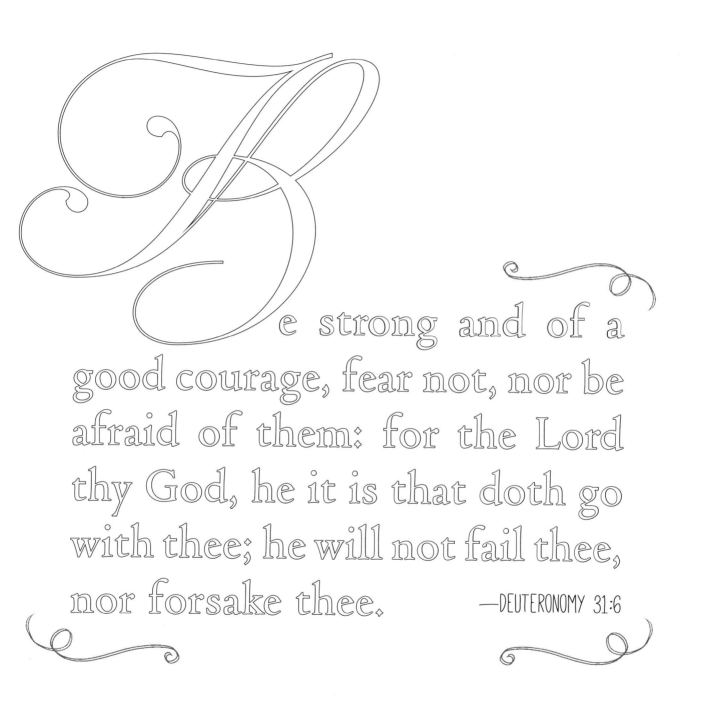

Be strong and of a good courage, fear not, nor be afraid of them: for the Lord thy God, he it is that doth go with thee; he will not fail thee, nor forsake thee.

—DEUTERONOMY 31:6

Illustration by Claudia Wolf

Be strong and of a good courage; be not afraid, neither be thou dismayed: Lord thy God is with thee whithersoever thou goest.

—JOSHUA 1:9

The Walls of Jericho · Illustration by Tammie Trucchi

As for me and my house, we will serve the Lord.

—JOSHUA 24:15

I will NEVER BREAK MY COVENANT with you.

—JUDGES 2:1

Jael and Sisera · Illustration by Tammie Trucchi

WHITHER THOU GOEST, *I will go;* AND WHERE THOU LODGEST, *I will lodge:* THY PEOPLE SHALL BE MY PEOPLE, *and thy God* MY GOD.

—RUTH 1:16

Hannah's Prayer · Illustration by Tammie Trucchi

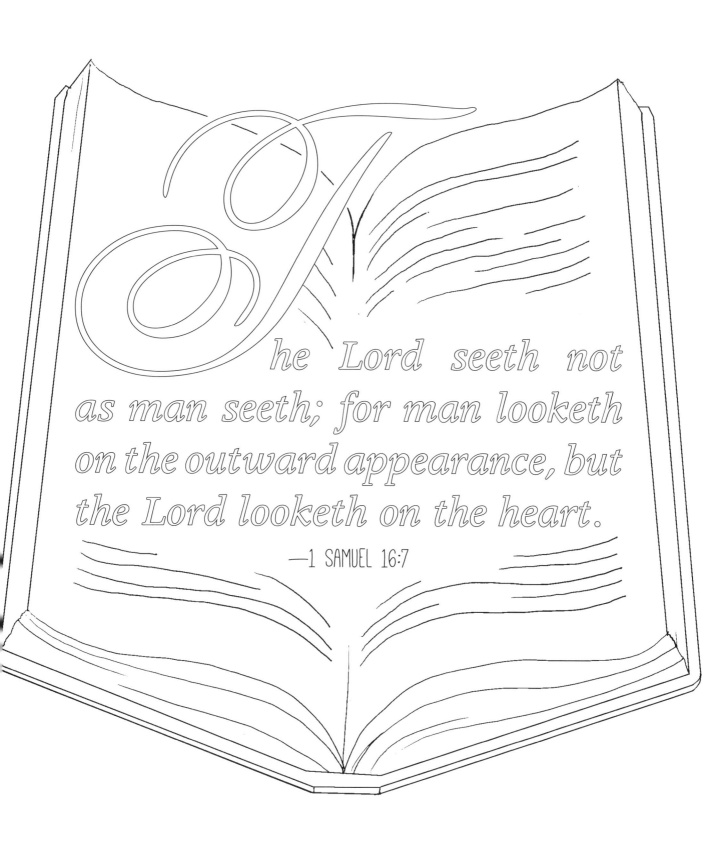

The Lord seeth not as man seeth; for man looketh on the outward appearance, but the Lord looketh on the heart.

—1 SAMUEL 16:7

David and Goliath · Illustration by Tammie Trucchi

David and Abigail · Illustration by Tammie Trucchi

Saul and the Witch of Endor · Illustration by Tammie Trucchi

The Ark Is Brought to Jerusalem · Illustration by Tammie Trucchi

David and Bathsheba · Illustration by Tammie Trucchi

The Death of Absalom · Illustration by Tammie Trucchi

The Fall of Jezebel · Illustration by Tammie Trucchi

Elijah and the Ravens · Illustration by Tammie Trucchi

The Blind Army · Illustration by Tammie Trucchi

THE **JOY** OF THE **Lord** IS YOUR *Strength.*

—NEHEMIAH 8:10

Who knoweth
whether
thou art come
to the kingdom
for such
a time as this?

—ESTHER 4:14

Queen Esther · *Illustration by Tammie Trucchi*

For I know that my redeemer liveth, and that he shall stand at the latter day upon the Earth. —JOB 19:25

I WILL BOTH
LAY ME DOWN IN
Peace,
AND SLEEP: FOR THOU,
Lord,
ONLY MAKEST ME
DWELL IN SAFETY.

—PSALM 4:8

CAST THY BURDEN
UPON THE LORD,
and he shall sustain thee:
HE SHALL NEVER SUFFER
the righteous to be moved.

—PSALM 55:22

He shall cover thee with his feathers, and under his wings shalt thou trust.

—PSALM 91:4

KEEP THY *Heart* with all diligence; FOR OUT OF IT ARE the issues OF LIFE.

—PROVERBS 4:23

Pleasant Words are as a Honeycomb, sweet to the soul, and health to the bones.

—PROVERBS 16:24

Strength
and honour
ARE HER CLOTHING;
AND
she shall
rejoice
IN TIME
TO COME.
—PROVERBS 31:25

He hath made every thing beautiful in his time. —ECCLESIASTES 3:11

Two are better than one.

—ECCLESIASTES 4:9

FEAR NOT: FOR I HAVE *Redeemed* ~ *thee* ~ I HAVE CALLED THEE BY THY NAME; THOU ART MINE.

—ISAIAH 43:1

FOR YE SHALL GO

out with joy, and be led forth with peace: the mountains and the hills shall break forth before you into singing, and all the trees of the field shall clap their hands.

—ISAIAH 55:12

Thou shalt be like a watered garden, and like a spring of water, whose waters fail not.

—ISAIAH 58:11

BLESSED
IS THE MAN THAT
TRUSTETH IN
THE LORD,
& WHOSE HOPE
THE LORD IS.

—JEREMIAH 17:7

And ye SHALL SEEK ME, *and find me,* WHEN YE SHALL SEARCH FOR ME *with all your* Heart.

—JEREMIAH 29:13

Yea, I have loved
thee with an everlasting

Love;

therefore
with
loving kindness
have I drawn thee.

—JEREMIAH 31:3

Call unto me,
and I will answer thee,
and show thee
Great
AND
MIGHTY THINGS,
which thou knowest not.

—JEREMIAH 33:3

Illustration by Claudia Wolf

I will hope in him.

—LAMENTATIONS 3:24

I will cause the Shower to come down in his season; there shall be Showers of Blessing.

—EZEKIEL 34:26

The Statue of Nebuchadnezzar · Illustration by Tammie Trucchi

The Fiery Furnace · Illustration by Tammie Trucchi

The Great Tree · Illustration by Tammie Trucchi

Daniel in the Lion's Den · Illustration by Tammie Trucchi

Daniel's Visions · Illustration by Tammie Trucchi

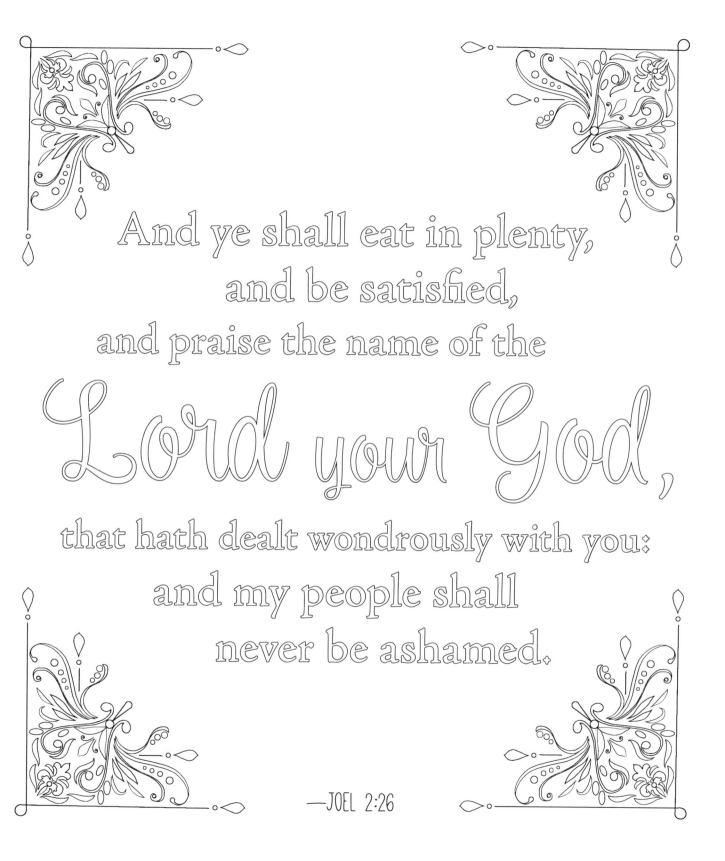

And ye shall eat in plenty,
and be satisfied,
and praise the name of the
Lord your God,
that hath dealt wondrously with you:
and my people shall
never be ashamed.

—JOEL 2:26

THE LION HATH ROARED, who will not fear? THE LORD GOD HATH SPOKEN, who can but prophesy?

—AMOS 3:8

Jonah and the Great Fish · Illustration by Tammie Trucchi

ABOUT THE ILLUSTRATORS

Tammie Trucchi was born and raised on the South Shore of Massachusetts. In 2002, she graduated from the School of the Museum of Fine Arts and Tufts University where she earned a bachelor's degree in fine art. While attending the SMFA, much of her studies focused on technical painting and works inspired by the Bible. Until now, her primary medium has been oil painting. She has always found coloring books to be inspiring as well as calming. In addition to countless books on art techniques and artist catalogues, one will always find an assortment of coloring books throughout her home.

Claudia Wolf graduated from the Paier College of Art and works as an illustrator, graphic designer, fine and portrait artist, and photographer in her Connecticut studio. She works extensively with airbrush, watercolors, acrylics, pastels, oils, and digital art. In addition to her work on book covers and interiors, Claudia has illustrated classic fairy tales such as *Hansel and Gretel* and *Snow White* as well as a wide range of other picture books for HarperCollins and McGraw-Hill. She is also a courtroom sketch artist. Her national assignments with ABC, NBC, FOX, and CNN prove to be exciting as well as challenging.